M000122066

SONGS OF THE CHRISTMAS STORY

TRADITIONAL CAROLS THAT TELL THE TRUE STORY OF JESUS' BIRTH

Loveland, Colorado

Group

Real. **Bold.** Love.

Group resources really work!

This Group resource incorporates our R.E.A.L. approach to ministry. It reinforces a growing friendship with Jesus, encourages long-term learning, and results in life transformation, because it's:

Relational—Learner-to-learner interaction enhances learning and builds Christian friendships.

Experiential—What learners experience through discussion and action sticks with them up to 9 times longer than what they simply hear or read.

Applicable—The aim of Christian education is to equip learners to be both hearers and doers of God's Word.

Learner-based—Learners understand and retain more when the learning process takes into consideration how they learn best.

Songs of the Christmas Story:
Traditional Carols That Tell the True Story of Jesus' Birth

Songs of the Christmas Story was created by the amazing and talented team at Group.

Credits
Editor: Charity Kauffman
Executive Editor: Jody Brolsma
Assistant Editor: Lyndsay Gerwing
Chief Creative Officer: Joani Schultz
Art Director: Veronica Preston
Production Designer: Shelly Dillon
Special thanks to Dave and Jess Ray from Doorpost Songs Family Worship.

Unless otherwise indicated, all Scripture quotations are taken from the *Holy Bible*, New Living Translation, copyright © 1996, 2004, 2007, 2013, 2015 by Tyndale House Foundation. Used by permission of Tyndale House Publishers, Inc., Carol Stream, Illinois 60188. All rights reserved.

ISBN 978-1-4707-5130-2

Printed in the U.S.A.

10 9 8 7 6 5 4 3 2 1   19 18 17

TABLE OF CONTENTS

INTRODUCTION

They're the soundtrack of the Christmas season. Christmas carols ring out at shopping malls, through radios, and on network TV specials. Choirs sing them, dancers bring them to life, and movies know when to cue them at just the right moment.

But the songs of Christmas provide more than holiday cheer. For hundreds of years, traditional carols have told the true story of Jesus' birth—and they have stories of their own to tell! Use these lessons to share the songs, the stories, and God's plan to send a Rescuer to the world that very first Christmas.

Each lesson weaves together Scripture, biblical context, hands-on experiences, discussion, history, and beloved Christmas songs. There's a little something for everyone! We've kept supplies simple so you can spend time building friendships with kids instead of prepping supplies.

And we're so excited for you to hear and sing along with four *brand-new* Christmas carol arrangements. Having heard their stories, you'll sing them in a whole new way—with your voice *and* your heart! They're available on DVD at the back of this book. You can also use the code to download the video and audio versions. Remember that these songs are copyrighted and for classroom use only. Please don't make copies to share with others.

You'll see that handouts and take-home pages *are* free to copy. You'll need them for some of the experiences and to share the songs of Christmas with families at home.

Here's an overview of what kids will discover:

WEEK	BIBLE POINT	BIBLE STORY	SONG
1	God has a plan.	Isaiah Talks About a Savior King (Isaiah 9:2-7)	"Joy to the World!"
2	God's plan is surprising.	Jesus Is Born in Bethlehem (Luke 2:1-7)	"Silent Night"
3	God's plan is for everyone.	The Angels Visit the Shepherds (Luke 2:8-14)	"Angels We Have Heard on High"
4	God's plan is something to celebrate.	The Shepherds Tell About Jesus' Birth (Luke 2:15-20; John 1:12, 14)	"O Come, All Ye Faithful"

We wish you a merry Christmas and great joy as you celebrate Jesus!

WEEK ONE:
JOY TO THE WORLD!

BIBLE POINT:

God has a plan.

KEY SCRIPTURE:

Isaiah Talks About a Savior King (Isaiah 9:2-7)

FOR LEADERS

Have you ever walked in darkness? Perhaps you've stubbed your toe on the way to your kitchen coffeepot before sunrise, or maybe you went through or are in the middle of a serious time of sadness or disappointment. Isaiah had a message for God's people who were walking in darkness: **God has a plan**; a light will come. And he did! In Jesus, God revealed his plan to save people from sin so we can be friends with God again. That friendship changes everything! Even in life's darkest moments, we find joy in Jesus, our Wonderful Counselor, Mighty God, Everlasting Father, and Prince of Peace.

Kids go through dark times, too. Even when surrounded by Christmas lights and cheer, kids face disappointments and fears. They, too, may wonder what God is up to when friends are mean, parents fight, or things don't go the way they want. Help your kids see how Jesus surprises us even in the darkest moments by bringing friendship to our hearts and joy to the world.

Read 2 Kings 17:5-21; 25:8-21 for the back story on how God's people found themselves in "darkness."

OVERVIEW

EXPERIENCES		ACTIVITIES	SUPPLIES
Get Started	10 minutes	Share favorite Christmas songs.	• smartphone or tablet (optional) • Bibles
Bible Discovery	10-15 minutes	**People Walking in Darkness**—Experience what it's like to walk in darkness.	• sunglasses (1 per child) • piece of Christmas candy • "Joy to the World!" music video
	10-15 minutes	**A Light Will Shine**—Uncover God's plan.	• Bibles • 5 battery-operated pillar or taper candles • removable tape • permanent markers • "And He Will Be Called" handout (1 per child) • pens or pencils
	10 minutes	**God's Plan Is Jesus**—See how Jesus is God's plan.	• pieces of Christmas candy (1 per child)
Music Video	3 minutes	Sing "Joy to the World!"	• "Joy to the World!" music video
Carol Story: "Joy to the World!"	10-15 minutes	Hear the story behind "Joy to the World!" and write song lyrics based on Isaiah 9:6.	• Bibles • paper (1 for every 2 kids) • pencils (1 for every 2 kids)
Life Application and Prayer	10-15 minutes	Consider making room for Jesus this Christmas season.	• multicolored card stock (1 per child) • red and white chenille wires (3 of each color per child) • Glue Dots • markers

⇨ GET STARTED

Welcome kids with music! Play and sing along with the "O Come, All Ye Faithful" and "Joy to the World!" music videos as kids gather.

Get kids talking with this icebreaker question.

Ask: **What's your favorite Christmas song?** If you want to, as kids mention songs, create a festive environment by using a smartphone or tablet to find and play some of their suggestions.

Say: **Christmas music brings cheer to the Christmas season. But sometimes sad things happen and we don't feel very joyful. Before Jesus' birth, God's people weren't feeling very merry and bright. But** <u>God had a plan</u> **that would change not just their mood but also the whole world! Today we'll discover how a prophet named Isaiah cheered up God's people, not with "Jingle Bells" but with God's promise of a Savior king.**

Help kids find the book of Isaiah in the Bible. Point out that it's in the middle of the Bible, so a lot had happened before and a lot was still to come, including Jesus's birth.

Isaiah was a prophet. That means he spoke messages from God. He reminded God's people about God's love but also about his rules. Isaiah warned people about what would happen if they ignored God and turned away from him. Isaiah spoke, but God's people didn't listen very well; sometimes it seems like they did the *opposite* **of what God said.**

Tell kids to imagine they are the Israelites. You will give them instructions, and they should do the opposite of what you say. Ask kids to:

- **Raise your right hand.**
- **Slouch in your chair.**
- **Close your eyes.**
- **Sit down.**

End so kids are all standing.

Say: **God's people didn't listen, and they got in big trouble. The book of 2 Kings in the Bible tells what happened. In 722 B.C. a powerful nation called Assyria took over the Northern Kingdom of Israel.**

Have kids in the back of the room sit down.

Then in 586 B.C. the Babylonians destroyed Jerusalem, and the people of Judah had to leave their homes.

Have the rest of the kids sit down.

Even after some of them returned, things were a mess.

Ask a few kids to stand back up, representing God's people who returned to Jerusalem.

God's people lost their land, their leaders, and their joy. Even though God had a plan, his people couldn't see it. It was like walking in darkness. Let's see how well *you* like walking in darkness.

🔎 BIBLE DISCOVERY

PEOPLE WALKING IN DARKNESS

Give each child a pair of sunglasses to wear, and turn off room lights. Discreetly put a piece of candy in your pocket and say that you've hidden a piece of candy somewhere in the room. Invite kids to walk around and look for it while wearing sunglasses. (You may need to offer some parameters.) Play "Joy to the World!" as they search (unsuccessfully). When the song ends, have kids return to their seats still wearing the sunglasses.

If you have a large class, have kids pair up, share sunglasses, and take turns searching. One partner will wear sunglasses and search while the other waits with eyes closed. Give partners 30 seconds at a time to search, and then have them swap roles for another 30 seconds, and so on until the song ends.

Ask: **Describe your search experience. How did sunglasses affect your view?**

Say: **Our room is typically a bright and happy place. But seen through dark lenses, it loses some of its brightness and joy.**

Isaiah spoke to discouraged people. God had promised to help them, but they couldn't see his plan. Like you wanted to find the candy quickly, God's people wanted a quick answer to their problem. But they couldn't find it.

Ask: **Why do you think we sometimes say hard times are dark times? When have you gone through a dark time?** Share an example from your own life to begin the conversation.

When we go through dark times, it can feel like no one is in control. That there's no way forward. That things are hopeless. But even in dark times, <u>God has a plan</u> for us!

A LIGHT WILL SHINE

Say: **Even though all seemed hopeless, God had a plan for the Israelites. So Isaiah kept talking. He told the people a special message: A Savior will come!** Turn the lights on, and have kids remove the sunglasses.

Read Isaiah 9:2-5.

Isaiah told the people God's plan—someone would help them and make things bright again.

Ask: **Who do you go to when you need help?** Share an example from your own life to begin the conversation.

Depending on the situation, people might ask for a parent or teacher's help. Maybe they'd call for a police officer or write a letter to their local government. Back then, God's people probably hoped that a mighty king or brave warrior would come defeat their enemies and get them out of trouble. But God had other ideas. Let's read to see who God would send to help.

Read Isaiah 9:6-7.

A *child* is born? Not a king or queen. Not a soldier or even a grown-up. God would send a child. But not just any child. He'd be an amazing Savior king who would help them. Let's explore the things Isaiah said about this child.

You'll need five battery-operated pillar or taper candles. Write each name mentioned in Isaiah 9:6 and the name "Jesus" on a separate piece of removable tape, and place one name on each candle. Save the "Jesus" candle for later.

- Wonderful Counselor
- Mighty God
- Everlasting Father
- Prince of Peace
- Jesus

Form four groups, and give each group a candle. Give each child a "And He Will Be Called" handout and a pen or pencil. Have kids work within their group to complete the handout using the name on their candle. Then turn off your room lights again, and have each group hold up its candle as group members share their name and responses. As each group shares, collect its candle in the middle of your space.

These candles bring light to our dark room, just like the child would bring light to a dark time.

Ask: **Which name brings *you* the most comfort and joy? Why?** Share your choice to begin the conversation.

GOD'S PLAN IS JESUS

Say: **Isaiah told people God's plan: A baby's birth would bring light and hope. And about 700 years later, it came true! Jesus—God's very own Son—was born. But Jesus wasn't just a king for the Israelites. He brought joy to the whole world.**

Add the candle that has "Jesus" on it.

God's plan didn't start with Isaiah's message. The plan began in the first book of the Bible, Genesis, when God's creation messed up and sin came into the world. Sin keeps people from being close to God. Throughout the whole Bible, people messed up again and again. No matter how hard they tried, or didn't try, sin ruined their friendship with God. But God's love is bigger than sin. He made a plan to get his friends back!

***Jesus* is God's plan to show the wonder of his love to the whole world. Jesus came unexpectedly, and he was found in a surprising place.** Reveal the piece of Christmas candy in your pocket, and welcome kids' reactions. **And he brought joy!** Distribute candy for children to enjoy.

God's plan is Jesus, **and we can make room for him! Not just in a nativity scene or on Christmas morning, but every day! We can prepare room in our hearts for Jesus. When we make room for Jesus, our eyes are opened to God's plan for *us*! But what does that look like?**

Ask: **Imagine you're going to stay at your friends' house for a few days. How might they prepare for your visit?**

Your friends might make a bed for you and buy your favorite breakfast cereal. But they probably wouldn't ignore you or leave you out of activities. Instead, they'd invite you along so you can have fun together.

When we prepare for a visitor, we're making room for that person in our lives. We can make room in our lives for Jesus, too.

Ask: **How could you make room for Jesus in your life? What might you get rid of?**

LET EVERY HEART PREPARE HIM ROOM.

When we make room for Jesus, we remember he's with us. We talk to him through prayer and listen to what he has to say as we read the Bible. We celebrate his friendship by singing songs that praise him, and we do things that make him happy, like showing love and helping people in need. When we make room for Jesus, we don't have room for other things. We might not yell at our family members or choose to watch a disrespectful show on TV. Instead, we fill our lives with things that bring joy!

God's plan is Jesus. He's the promised Savior king who brings joy to the world. Let's celebrate by singing a Christmas song!

 MUSIC VIDEO

Play the "Joy to the World!" music video, and encourage kids to sing along and do the motions. They'll really have a blast if you lead the way!

CAROL STORY: "JOY TO THE WORLD!"

Say: **Like the prophet Isaiah, Isaac Watts wanted to share God's message of hope with God-followers. He lived more than 300 years ago! Watts wanted to add some fresh creativity to church music. He wrote song lyrics based on verses from Psalms in the Old Testament of the Bible, but he loved to add the good news of Jesus from the New Testament, too.**

Read Psalm 98, and compare the psalm's words to the lyrics from "Joy to the World!"

At first people didn't know what to do with Isaac's newfangled lyrics. But when his

words were added to tunes written by George Frideric Handel, a famous composer who lived during that time, people loved it! That's how the song "Joy to the World!" was born. It wasn't originally written for Christmas, but people especially liked singing it to celebrate Jesus' birth.

Form pairs, and give each pair a piece of paper and a pencil.

Have kids rewrite Isaiah 9:6 in modern-day language. Challenge them to take it a step further and add their words to a favorite tune to create a brand-new worship song! Ask for volunteers to share their songs.

LIFE APPLICATION AND PRAYER

Say: **Your songs brought so much joy. We can look around and see lights and hear music everywhere at Christmas. But there are still people going through dark and difficult times. They really need joy from Jesus. They need to remember that <u>God has a plan</u> for them, too!**

Ask: **With whom can you share joy this Christmas?** Share an example from your own life to begin. Perhaps you plan to make a special present for a friend who's going through a hard time or participate in a service project to help people in your community.

Have kids make a joyful, encouraging card for someone who is going through a dark and difficult time.

Distribute three red and three white chenille wires to each child, and have kids twist each red wire with a white wire so they look like candy canes. Then have kids form the twists into the letters "J," "O," and "Y."

Have each child fold a piece of colored card stock in half to make a card and then use Glue Dots to attach the letters to the outside of the card. Invite each child to write an encouraging note to someone on the inside.

Be sure to plan how and when you'll give your card to someone in need of joy this week. You never know how Jesus can use your words to show his love.

Provide time for kids to pray for the people to whom they plan to give their cards, and then close in prayer, thanking God for his plan to send Jesus to be our Wonderful Counselor, Mighty God, Everlasting Father, and Prince of Peace.

If time remains, keep singing! We recommend "Silent Night" or "Angels We Have Heard on High."

🏠 TAKE IT HOME

Distribute the take-home page for this lesson to each child, or email the page to families.

AND HE WILL BE CALLED

HELLO! MY NAME IS _____.

Complete these sentences based on what you think someone with that name would be like.

I like to...

I will help you...

You might need me when you...

DISCOVER

God has a plan.

READ

Isaiah 9:2-7

Isaiah had a message for God's people who were walking in darkness: **God has a plan**; a light will come. And he did! In Jesus, God revealed his plan to save people from sin so we can be friends with God again. That friendship changes everything! Even in life's darkest moments, we find joy in Jesus, our Wonderful Counselor, Mighty God, Everlasting Father, and Prince of Peace.

SHARE

Gather your family in a room in your house. Turn off the lights, and have someone hold a flashlight as he or she reads the following question. The flashlight represents Jesus, the Light that came at Christmas.

First tell about a sad or dark day in your life, and then tell about a really happy or joyful day.

The person holding the flashlight goes first and then passes it to someone else. Give everyone a turn to shine light in the darkness as they share.

PRAY

When everyone has shared, pray and thank Jesus for bringing joy to the world.

LISTEN

Count the number of times you randomly hear "Joy to the World!" this week. It may be on your car radio or music you hear in stores or on TV. You can keep track on a phone or notebook. You'll listen for different songs this Christmas season and see which one is most popular!

SONGS OF THE CHRISTMAS STORY

SONG LYRICS
"JOY TO THE WORLD"

Oh, oh
Oh, oh
Oh, oh

Joy to the world!
The Lord is come!
Let earth receive her King!
Let every heart prepare him room,
And heaven and nature sing,
And heaven and nature sing,
And heaven, and heaven, and nature sing.

Oh, oh
Oh, oh
Oh, oh

He rules the world
with truth and grace,
And makes the nations prove
The glories of his righteousness,
And wonders of his love,
And wonders of his love,

And wonders, wonders of his love.

Oh, oh
Oh, oh
Oh, oh

Joy to the world!
The Lord is come!
Let earth receive her King!
Let every heart prepare him room,
And heaven and nature sing,
And heaven and nature sing,
And heaven, and heaven, and nature sing.

Oh, oh
Oh, oh
Oh, oh

"Joy to the World!" by George F. Handel.

WEEK TWO:

SILENT NIGHT

BIBLE POINT:

God's plan is surprising.

KEY SCRIPTURE:

Jesus Is Born in Bethlehem (Luke 2:1-7)

FOR LEADERS

You've made your lists and checked them twice. The calendar is updated with parties, concerts, and church services. Then, surprise! Your water heater stops working the day relatives get to town. Surprise! Concerts are canceled and rescheduled. Surprise! A family member gets sick on the way to the Christmas Eve service. This may not be what you planned, but God's still at work.

Kids seem to like surprises…if they're good. But changes in routines can unsettle them, too. Use this lesson to help kids discover that God is quietly at work, even when things don't go the way we plan or expect. **God's plan is surprising**! His surprises can actually draw us closer to him and show us how much he loves us.

God often works in unexpected ways. As you prepare for this lesson, think back to other stories in the Bible that show when God chose unlikely people or situations to do amazing things. Examples include Joseph (Genesis 37–45), Gideon (Judges 6–7), David (1 Samuel 16), and Esther (Esther 2–9).

OVERVIEW

EXPERIENCES		ACTIVITIES	SUPPLIES
Get Started	15 minutes	Share surprising moments and shake up a surprising discovery.	• can of clear, regular soda (Sprite or club soda works well) • sink or trash can
Bible Discovery	10 minutes	**What's That Sound?**—Identify noises that tell you something.	• smartphone or tablet
	10-15 minutes	**Hometown Bound**—Play a game where kids will "register" in their hometowns.	• Bibles • poster board (1 for every 6 kids) • markers
	10 minutes	**Jesus Is Born**—Read about the day Jesus was born.	• Bibles
Music Video	3 minutes	Sing "Silent Night."	• "Silent Night" music video
Carol Story: "Silent Night"	10-15 minutes	Hear the story behind "Silent Night," and make a guitar.	• 16-ounce cups (3 per child) • rubber bands (assorted colors, weights, and sizes) (7 per child) • Christmas stickers, wrapping-paper pieces, washi tape, or other materials (optional)
Life Application and Prayer	10-15 minutes	Talk to God about expected and surprising things in your life.	

⇨ GET STARTED

Welcome kids with music! Play and sing along with the "Joy to the World!" and "Silent Night" music videos as kids gather.

Get kids talking with this icebreaker question.

Ask: **When have you been surprised? What did you think would happen instead?** Share an example from your own life to begin the conversation.

Say: **The Christmas story in the Bible bursts with surprises. "Mary, you're going to have a baby." Surprise! "*God* is the father." Add an unexpected road trip, no available guest rooms, and a feeding trough for a cradle, and you have one amazing birthday!**

These may have seemed like surprising events, but each twist and turn was part of God's plan. <u>God's plan is surprising</u>! We can trust that God is in control, even when he does things we don't expect. Before we dive into the story, let's begin with a surprising experiment.

Be sure to practice this activity beforehand to build your confidence. You'll find that the more you tap the sides, the better it works.

Show kids a can of clear, regular (not diet) soda. (Club soda or Sprite works well.)

Ask: **What do you expect will happen if we shake up this can of soda and then open it?** Invite kids' responses.

Say: **We expect that it'll spray everywhere, right? I've seen that happen before. Have you? Let's give it a try!**

Have kids pass the unopened soda can around so everyone has a turn to give it a good shake. Then have kids pass the soda back to you to open it.

Hold the soda can over a sink or trash can, as if preparing for a big explosion. But before you open it, use your fingers to snap or tap the side of the can. Tap all the way around several times. This moves the air bubbles from the side to the top of the can. After tapping, open the can. Gas will escape, but no (or not much) liquid!

Surprise! The soda didn't react the way we thought it would. It's surprising because we've seen soda explode before, but things were different this time. We might have

expected a loud burst, but we only got a quiet pop. A few taps made a difference.

Ask: **When have you experienced a not-so-good surprise?** Share an example from your own life to begin the conversation. Perhaps you got a flat tire on the first day of vacation, or maybe you were let go from your job at work.

Ask: **When did a surprise lead to something even better than you expected?** Share an example from your own life. Perhaps leaving one job led to another one where you met your best friend, or when you stopped to fix the tire you found a really great ice cream shop.

Sometimes surprises bring excitement, but other times they leave us feeling a little puzzled. <u>God's plan is surprising</u>. His plan to send a Rescuer was different from what most people were expecting, but it changed the world forever...in a good way!

 BIBLE DISCOVERY

WHAT'S THAT SOUND?

Say: **In the Old Testament of the Bible, the prophet Isaiah told God's people that a Savior king would come make things better. But for Mary, Joseph, and the rest of God's people, it was 700 years later and no Rescuer had come to help them. They were still waiting.**

Ask: **Imagine what a king looks like. What do you think God's people were waiting to see or hear?**

Use a smartphone or tablet to play a simple royal trumpet call. *(Do do-do doo!)*

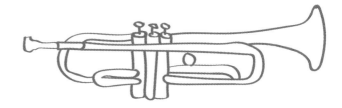

At different times in the Old Testament, leaders of God's people would blow horns or trumpets to signal something special. You may have even seen movies about kings whose loyal subjects blew trumpets when their royal leader arrived.

We don't serve or live under a king's rule today. But we might recognize other sounds that let us know something is happening. Tell me what you think is about to happen based on these sounds.

Use your smartphone or tablet to play songs or jingles that communicate something. Have kids identify each sound and say what they tell us. Examples include:

- alarm clock

- doorbell
- "NFL on Fox" theme song
- Disney movie intro ("When You Wish Upon a Star")

These different sounds all have something in common. They alert us to something that's about to happen. Review what each sound tells you. For example, alarm clocks tell you to wake up, a doorbell alerts you to someone at the door, and theme songs let you know the show is about to begin.

Ask: **If you could create a sound effect for Jesus' birth, what would it sound like?** Form groups, and have kids in each group work together to invent a noise or tune and then share it with the whole group. You could even record the sounds and play them back for kids to hear themselves.

HOMETOWN BOUND

Say: **No sound effect signaled Jesus' arrival. The only thing people heard was a decree from Caesar Augustus, the emperor, or king, of Rome. After an angel appeared and said that Mary would give birth to the Son of God, Mary and Joseph waited for his birth. They probably expected the baby to be born at their home in Nazareth, surrounded by family to help. But God had other plans. Surprise!**

Read Luke 2:1-3.

Mary and Joseph got a surprise trip to Bethlehem, just when it was coming time for the baby to be born. Since Caesar Augustus was king of the Roman empire, *he* was in charge of God's people. If he said they needed to be counted, then off they went. Let's play a game where you'll register in your hometowns, too!

Form teams of no more than six kids. Have each team use the second letter of each person's first name to create the name of their team's imaginary hometown. (For example, Sarah, Ben, Elizabeth, Bobby, and Chloe's hometown might be "Aleho.")

Have each team write the name of its hometown on a piece of poster board and place it on the floor on the opposite side of the room. Start with all kids away from their "hometowns." On "go," one person from each team should grab a marker, run to the team's hometown sign, write the first letter of his or her name, and then race back and pass the marker to the next person on the team. That person will run and write the first letter of his or her name somewhere else on the sign. Teams continue racing back and forth until all members have written their complete names on the paper. Have kids cheer for each other until every child's name has been written and all kids have been "registered" in their hometowns.

It looks like we're all registered in *our* hometowns. Let's read to see where Mary and Joseph went.

Read Luke 2:4-5.

Surprise! Joseph and Mary had to go to Bethlehem. It wasn't the best place. Bethlehem was 70 miles away from Nazareth. Give kids an example of something that's about 70 miles from where you live so they have some context for the distance. **Walking there would have taken a week or two. It wasn't the best time, either. The Bible says Mary was obviously pregnant—the baby was coming soon! Mary had probably planned to spend that time at home preparing to be a mom. Instead, she and Joseph were off to Bethlehem.**

Bethlehem wasn't just Joseph's hometown; it was King David' hometown, too. King David had been Israel's best and most godly king. Perhaps that fact sounded a tiny alarm in Joseph and Mary's minds. Kings come from Bethlehem! Let's see what happened in Bethlehem.

JESUS IS BORN

Read Luke 2:6-7.

Say: **Christ, the Savior, was born. Earlier in Luke, an angel had told Mary something special about her baby. Listen to this:**

Read Luke 1:35.

This baby was holy. That means Jesus was special, set apart, and different from others. He wasn't just the son of Mary; he was the Son of God. This little baby was God's love for us wrapped up in strips of cloth, sleeping in a manger. Surprise!

It may have seemed ordinary, but that day (or night) was holy, too. It was the day God picked to become human. What a gift! Because Jesus was born, he knows what it's like to live on earth. Jesus was born like we were born. He cried like we cry. He

got hungry and tired like we do. He knows what it's like to have friends because he had some, too. He knows what it's like to be happy and sad. He knows what a hug feels like. Christmas day is holy because it gave us a best friend.

Ask: **How does it help you to know that you and Jesus have a lot in common? Why do you think God planned for Jesus to be born quietly in Bethlehem instead of in a palace with a loud celebration?**

Jesus' birth was surprising because people expected a Rescuer to come in a big, flashy way. But there was no ceremony or announcement made on TV or social media. No trumpets or theme songs. Other than the sounds of hungry animals and tired travelers, it was quiet when Jesus came. It was God's plan all along. <u>God's plan is surprising</u>.

Let's sing a song that describes Jesus' birth. The words help us imagine that surprising birthday.

 MUSIC VIDEO

Play and sing along with the "Silent Night" music video, and encourage kids to sing along and do the motions. They'll really have a blast if you lead the way!

📖 CAROL STORY: "SILENT NIGHT"

Say: **Organs are pretty loud instruments. They have blowers and keys and pipes that make a lot of sound. Two hundred years ago, most churches in Europe had big, beautiful organs that filled the air with music for people to sing along to. A village church in Oberndorf, Austria, was no different.**

But for some reason, Joseph Mohr, one of the church leaders, asked a local musician and schoolteacher named Franz Gruber to write a melody to his Christmas poem with a guitar, not an organ. Some people think the church organ was broken. There are even stories that mice had chewed the inside! No matter the reason, Franz wrote a melody for Joseph's poem called "Silent Night, Holy Night!" The loud organ stayed silent on Christmas Eve of 1818 as Joseph and Franz sang the song with a guitar.

Guitars are pretty quiet instruments. You strum or pluck the strings, and the tiny vibrations make a beautiful sound. You'll hear guitar music if you're sitting around a campfire with friends, but if you go to a concert, you'll probably see guitars plugged in to sound systems so people can hear better.

Ask: **Do you think Jesus' birth is more like an organ or a guitar? Why?**

The first performance of "Silent Night" was similar to the night Jesus was born. There wasn't a loud celebration, and it wasn't what people expected, but it gave us a Gift to love. Let's make our own guitars to remind us that <u>God's plan is surprising</u>.

Give each child three 16-ounce plastic cups and seven rubber bands in various sizes.

Start by stacking two cups. Then stretch six rubber bands (for a six-string guitar) over the cups to make "strings" over the opening. Secure the bands by stretching one more rubber band around the outside at the top of the cups. Show kids how to spread out the rubber bands so it's easier to pluck each one. Encourage kids to listen to each pitch and use their creativity as they order the different-sized bands. Generally, wider bands will make lower notes and smaller band will sound higher, but increasing or decreasing the tension of certain bands will also impact the sound.

Encourage kids to decorate the outside of the third cup, using stickers, wrapping-paper strips, washi tape, or other materials. Then place the "guitar" inside the third cup to secure and cover the bands.

Create your own Christmas concert, singing "Silent Night," "Joy to the World!" and other favorite carols with your guitars.

 # LIFE APPLICATION AND PRAYER

Say: **Was it really silent the night Jesus was born? Probably not. The streets may have been noisy with people and animals coming and going. And we don't even know that Jesus was born at night! But no matter the actual noise level, Jesus came quietly. So quietly that God's people, who had been waiting and watching for years, didn't even know it. What a surprise! <u>God's plan is surprising</u>, and he has surprising plans for us, too.**

Guide kids in the following closing prayer.

Tell God about a hard or sad thing that unexpectedly happened recently. Share examples to spark their thoughts. Perhaps they missed the bus to school, lost a basketball game, or discovered a cavity when they went to the dentist.

Thank God for being with you and helping you.

Tell God about something you're looking forward to this week. Share examples to spark their thoughts. Perhaps they have a Christmas party at school, a friend is coming to play, or they plan to go to their favorite restaurant. **Thank God for being with you and helping you.**

Let's be silent and listen to what God might have to say to us today. Wait for about a minute, or until kids get a little restless, and then close in prayer, thanking God for sending his Son to be our Savior.

If time remains, keep singing! We recommend "Angels We Have Heard on High" or "O Come, All Ye Faithful."

 TAKE IT HOME

Distribute the take-home page for this lesson to each child, or email the page to families.

DISCOVER

God's plan is surprising.

READ

Luke 2:1-7

The Christmas story in the Bible bursts with surprises. "Mary, you're going to have a baby." Surprise! "*God* is the father." Add an unexpected road trip, no available guest rooms, and a feeding trough for a cradle, and you have one amazing birthday!

These may have seemed like surprising events, but each twist and turn was part of God's plan. **God's plan is surprising**! We can trust that God is in control, even when he works quietly and does things we don't expect.

SHARE

Plan a quiet surprise for someone. Deliver hot chocolate to a friend at work, make and send a Christmas card to someone who lives far away, or drop off Christmas cookies for an elderly friend who lives alone. Don't make a big fuss—just quietly share Jesus' love. After you're finished, talk about this:

What quiet surprise would *you* like to receive from someone?

PRAY

When everyone has shared, pray and thank God that he's quietly at work in our lives.

LISTEN

Count the number of times you randomly hear "Silent Night" this week. It may be on your car radio or music you hear in stores or on TV. You can keep track on a phone or notebook. You'll listen for different songs this Christmas season and see which one is most popular!

SONG LYRICS
"SILENT NIGHT"

Silent night, holy night,

All is calm, all is bright

'Round yon virgin mother and child.

Holy infant, so tender and mild,

Sleep in heavenly peace,

Sleep in heavenly peace.

Silent night, holy night,

Son of God, love's pure light.

Radiant beams from thy holy face,

With the dawn of redeeming grace,

Jesus, Lord at thy birth.

Jesus, Lord at thy birth.

"Silent Night" by Josef Mohr.

WEEK THREE:
ANGELS WE HAVE HEARD ON HIGH

BIBLE POINT:

God's plan is for everyone.

KEY SCRIPTURE:

The Angels Visit the Shepherds (Luke 2:8-14)

FOR LEADERS

Who have you praised lately? We may find ourselves cheering at a sporting event or clapping enthusiastically after a musician's beautiful rendition of a Christmas classic. In these and other instances, we're honoring something good. We give glory to our favorite players and artists for touchdowns and melodies, but imagine a praise party sparked by news of a Savior! The angels gave God glory that first Christmas, and the countryside resounded with radiant praise.

Kids are used to clapping, cheering, or praising people they admire. Use this lesson to help them point glory to God and his plan to show his amazing love. His plan isn't just for famous people who get a lot of attention—**God's plan is for everyone**! Kids can praise God for sending Jesus because he's a gift for them, too.

Shepherds don't debut in the Christmas story. In fact, shepherding is a profession referenced throughout the Bible. As you prepare for this lesson, revisit Psalm 23. A former shepherd, King David, wrote this familiar psalm as a way to glorify and honor the Good Shepherd. Read it as a prayer, and thank Jesus for guiding you as you care for his children.

OVERVIEW

EXPERIENCES		ACTIVITIES	SUPPLIES
Get Started	10 minutes	Share about favorite "stars."	
Bible Discovery	15 minutes	**Shepherds and Sheep—**Pretend to be shepherds and sheep.	• bandannas (1 for every 2 kids) • dark-colored circle stickers (1 for every 2 kids)
	10-15 minutes	**In the Spotlight—**Hear the angel's message to the shepherds.	• Bibles • flashlight or portable spotlight
	10-15 minutes	**Gloria!—**Create a scratch-art drawing to depict the heavenly host of angels.	• Bibles • plastic tablecloths or wax paper • card stock (1 per child) • crayons or oil pastels • black tempera paint • paintbrushes • cotton swabs or toothpicks (1 per child) • "Angels We Have Heard on High" music video
Music Video	3 minutes	Sing "Angels We Have Heard on High."	• "Angels We Have Heard on High" music video
Carol Story: "Angels We Have Heard on High"	10 minutes	Find out how "Angels We Have Heard on High" comes from many people and languages.	• world map or globe
Life Application and Prayer	10-15 minutes	Give God glory for things he's done for you.	• paper or foam stars • tape • fishing line

 GET STARTED

Welcome kids with music! Play and sing along with the "Silent Night" and "Angels We Have Hear on High" music videos as kids gather.

Get kids talking with this icebreaker question.

Ask: **Who is your favorite sports, TV, or movie star? Why do you like him or her?** Tell about a favorite athlete or actor you like to begin the conversation.

Say: **We give well-known people praise and honor. We clap when they make a layup, or we give them awards. We might even call them stars! That's what giving glory means—we cheer for them and honor them for their greatness.**

That's what a heavenly host of angels did when Jesus was born. They gave God glory for sending Jesus, the Rescuer! Who got to see this all-star show? Lowly shepherds got front-row seats. God's plan isn't just for people we think are the most talented or important. <u>God's plan is for everyone</u>!

 BIBLE DISCOVERY

SHEPHERDS AND SHEEP

Say: **Let's set the scene for today's Bible story when the angels told the shepherds about Jesus' birth.**

Read Luke 2:8.

Let's re-create that scene.

Choose half the kids to be shepherds and the other half sheep. Give shepherds bandannas to tie around their heads, and give sheep dark circle stickers to place on their noses. In a spacious area of your room, have shepherds and sheep re-enact a typical day of shepherding. Include activities like:

- Wake up in the morning.
- Find a stream and get water.
- Take sheep to a grassy area.
- Avoid places where wolves hang out.
- Find lost sheep.

Once sheep and shepherds are in character, narrate this scene.

It was an ordinary night. After a long day of looking for safe pastures and finding water for their woolly friends, the shepherds had counted and recounted the flock, built a sheepfold from nearby rocks, and settled in for the night.

Some shepherds may stand and pretend to keep an eye out for dangerous animals. Others might pretend to sleep. Sheep may pretend to sleep or eat grass from the "field."

Your average shepherd didn't get much glory back in the day, but some famous people started out as shepherds. In fact, famous shepherds can be found throughout the Old Testament. Jacob got rich from being a shepherd, and he met his future wife, Rachel, when she was watering sheep. Moses led sheep before he led people. And David, the giant slayer and mighty king, began his career as a shepherd who fought off lions and bears.

Encourage shepherds to stand tall and proud and sheep to "baa" happily, as if cheering for the shepherds.

But something had changed over the years. During the time Jesus was born, shepherds weren't famous or popular anymore. They were lower-class citizens whose biggest fans were probably sheep.

Ask: **Turn to a partner and tell about a boring job you have to do. Is there a chore or task you wish you could do instead?** Share an example from your own life to start the conversations.

Important people may have looked down on shepherds, but sheep were like their groupies who knew their shepherds' voices and followed them. Shepherds, let's play a little game to see if these sheep know your voices.

Pair each shepherd with a sheep. Invite shepherds to turn to their sheep and say, "Here, [sheep's name], follow me." Have shepherds repeat this statement a couple of times so sheep grow accustomed to their shepherds' voices.

Have shepherds tie their bandannas around their sheep's eyes like a blindfold and then stand across the room from them while sheep crouch on their hands and knees. (Or simply have crouching sheep close their eyes and promise not to peek.) Make sure shepherds are scattered and not standing directly across from their sheep.

On "go," sheep must crawl forward and try to find their shepherds by listening for their voices. The shepherds will stand and repeat, "Here, [sheep's name], follow me." The first sheep to find his or her shepherd wins.

Well done! Let's return to our "field" and hear about the glory-filled show.

IN THE SPOTLIGHT

Have sheep and shepherds gather back in the "field" again, and turn off the classroom lights to represent nighttime.

With the lights off, read Luke 2:9-12 slowly and with expression, giving kids' eyes time to adjust to the darkness. You may need a small reading light to help you see.

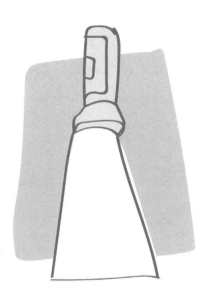

Ask: **When have you or a family member turned on a light in the middle of the night? How did your eyes react?**

Say: **It's shocking, isn't it? In the dark, your pupils are big and not prepared to see bright lights. Let's see how our eyes react right now.** Count to three, and then turn the classroom lights back on. Encourage kids' reactions to the light.

The Bible says that the "radiance of the Lord's glory" surrounded the shepherds. It's like the field was a dark stage and the Lord's glory was a spotlight that showed something special.

Ask: **Tell about a time you or someone you know stood on stage in the spotlight. What was it like?** Share an example from your own life to begin the conversation.

Standing in the spotlight makes many people nervous and scared—that's why some people get something called "stage fright." The shepherds had "field fright"! They probably weren't used to being in the spotlight. Let's see if you are.

With shepherds and sheep still in the "field," shine a light on every person (like on a stage or runway). When the light shines on each child, invite that child to say his or her name and one thing he or she likes to do. Invite kids to clap for their friends. After their turn in the spotlight, have kids return to their seats. Be sure to direct the flashlight or spotlight above each person and at an angle to avoid shining light directly in kids' eyes.

Once everyone is seated, remind kids what the angels said.

Let's read again what the angel said to help the shepherds' field fright.

Ask a volunteer to read Luke 2:10-12.

Because <u>God's plan is for everyone</u>, simple shepherds met a glorious angel who gave good news of great joy. The promised Rescuer had come, and shepherds were the first to know. Let's keep reading and see what happened next.

GLORIA!

Read Luke 2:13-14.

Ask: **When you picture this scene from the Christmas story, what do you imagine it looked like?** Mention your own thoughts to begin. Perhaps you think of Christmas choir scenes from movies or pictures you've seen in Bible storybooks.

Encourage kids to create their own scenes that include angels, shepherds, and sheep on homemade scratch-art paper.

Begin by covering tables with plastic tablecloths, or give each child a large piece of wax paper to catch stray strokes. Give each child a piece of card stock. Have each child color the entire sheet of card stock with brightly colored crayons or oil pastels. Once the page is completely covered, have kids brush one or two coats of black tempera paint over the whole thing. It's okay if some crayon still shows through.

Last, have kids use cotton swabs or toothpicks to create the scene from Luke 2:13-14. Play "Angels We Have Heard on High" as kids design their scratch art.

(You may choose to save time and avoid some mess by purchasing premade scratch-art paper online or at a local office supply store.)

As pictures dry, lead this discussion to wrap up the Bible story.

GLORIA! IN EXCELSIS DEO

Say: **Like the colors in your paintings showed through the dark paint, the vast armies of heaven burst through the night sky to give honor and praise to God. That's what "Gloria in excelsis Deo" [Glawr-ee-uh in ex-shell-cease dey-oh] means—"glory to God in the highest" in a language called Latin. The angels lit up the sky with God's glory and shone a heavenly spotlight on how awesome he is.**

Ask: **When have you seen God's glory on display?** Share a story from your own life. Perhaps you saw God's awesomeness in a sunset or freshly fallen snow. Or maybe you realized how great he is through a baby's birth or a time he healed you or a friend.

We give glory to God when we praise him for what he's done. The angels gave glory to God. They didn't praise the shepherds for being the first to hear. They didn't applaud Mary and Joseph for being good parents. They didn't praise themselves for an award-worthy performance. The angels gave glory to the only One who deserves it, God.

God's plan to save the world from sin was born, and he chose to tell shepherds first.

Ask: **Why do you think God started with shepherds? If Jesus were born today instead of 2000 years ago, who do you think should be the first to hear about it?**

We might think the news reporters or TV news anchors should be the first to know so they could spread the word. Or maybe world leaders or famous pastors should hear it first.

So many people in our world today need to hear about Jesus. Celebrities need Jesus. So do criminals, politicians, teachers, pastors, and kids like you. We all need Jesus because we all have sin. We all choose our own way over God's way. That's why God is so amazing. <u>God's plan is for everyone</u>. He doesn't pick favorites or love some people more than others. He sees our best and our worst and loves us anyway. That's why we praise him and give him glory. It's like we're shining a light on how awesome he is! Let's do that right now by singing the words that the angels said in front of the shepherds.

🎵 MUSIC VIDEO

Play the "Angels We Have Heard on High" music video, and encourage kids to sing along and do the motions. They'll really have a blast if you lead the way!

📖 CAROL STORY: "ANGELS WE HAVE HEARD ON HIGH"

Ask: **How can we say hello in other languages?** Encourage kids to share what they know, and mention several options, such as "Hola" in Spanish, "Bonjour" in French, and "Aloha" in Hawaiian.

Say: **When Jesus was born, most people spoke Aramaic or Greek. Then the Romans took over and introduced the Latin language.**

"Gloria in excelsis Deo" is a Latin phrase that means "Glory to God in the highest." So when we sing "Angels We Have Heard on High," we're singing Latin!

"Angels We Have Heard on High" has gone through a lot of translations! Its story reminds us that <u>God's plan is for everyone</u>! I'll show you what I mean with this map.

Show kids a world map or globe. Point to each area as you tell the story sequence.

Point to Israel. Say: **The shepherds heard the angels praise God in a language they understood. Jesus was born here.**

Point to Greece. Say: **Later, Luke wrote the Christmas story in Greek so the new Christians could hear about Jesus' birth.**

Point to Italy. Say: **Then the message was translated into Latin—"Gloria in excelsis Deo." Christianity became really important in Rome, and many churches were built there.**

Point to France. Say: **Hundreds of years later, "Glory to God in the highest" was part of a French Christmas carol that told the story of the angels visiting the shepherds. It was called "Les Anges dans Nos Campagnes," which means "Angels in Our Fields."**

Point to England. Say: **A church leader named James Chadwick lived in England. He heard the French carol and translated the words into English.**

Point to the United States. Say: **Then about 80 years ago, in 1937, an American organist named Edward Shippen Barnes wrote a tune for James' translation, making it a Christmas carol for American churches.**

Point all over the map. Say: **And people all over the world give God glory as they sing this song at Christmastime! Just like this song was translated over and over for more** and more people, <u>God's plan is for everyone</u>. "Angels We Have Heard on High" helps us all celebrate Jesus.

LIFE APPLICATION AND PRAYER

Say: **The angels told the shepherds that Jesus was born, and they lit up the sky giving God glory. We may not see a vast heavenly army in the sky today, but we can look up and see shining stars that remind us of our great God who sent Jesus to rescue us from sin. Thanks to Jesus, God is with us every day, shining love into our lives.**

Give each child a paper star, and encourage kids to write a sentence or two that praises God. They could thank God for who he is (our Creator, Friend, Helper) or what he's done (helped us feel better, helped us with a test at school, given us people to love).

Tape stars to the top of a wall or hang them from the ceiling with fishing line. Then encourage kids to reach toward the stars, as if cheering for God, and say together, "Glory to God in the highest! Amen."

If time remains, keep singing! We recommend "Joy to the World!" or "O Come, All Ye Faithful."

TAKE IT HOME

Distribute the take-home page for this lesson to each child, or email the page to families.

TAKE IT HOME
"ANGELS WE HAVE HEARD ON HIGH"

DISCOVER

God's plan is for everyone.

READ

Luke 2:8-14

We give famous people praise and honor. We clap when they make a layup, or we give them awards. We might even call them stars! That's what giving glory means—we cheer and honor somebody for greatness.

That's what a heavenly host of angels did when Jesus was born. They gave God glory for sending Jesus—the Rescuer—and lowly shepherds got front-row seats. God's plan isn't just for people we think are the most talented or important; **God's plan is for everyone**!

SHARE

Cheer for God at home this week when you notice ways your family members praise him with their lives. For example, when Bobby builds a cool Lego car, say "Thank you, God, for Bobby's creativity!" Or when Mom or Dad makes a delicious dinner, say "Thank you, God, that Mom and Dad take good care of us." Praise God for working through each person in your family. Talk about this question:

Imagine that, like the angels, you're God's messengers. What message needs to be told today? Who would you tell?

PRAY

When everyone has shared, praise God for sending Jesus to be our Savior. Tell him he's amazing!

LISTEN

Count the number of times you randomly hear "Angels We Have Heard on High" this week. It may be on your car radio or music you hear in stores or on TV. You can keep track on a phone or notebook. You'll listen for different songs this Christmas season and see which one is most popular!

Group
Real. Bold. Love.

SONG LYRICS
"ANGELS WE HAVE HEARD ON HIGH"

Angels we have heard on high
Sweetly singing o'er the plains,
And the mountains in reply
Echoing their joyous strains.

Gloria in excelsis Deo!

Come to Bethlehem, and see
Him whose birth the angels sing;
Come, adore on bended knee
Christ the Lord, our newborn King.

Gloria in excelsis Deo!
Gloria in excelsis Deo!

We sing gloria.
We sing gloria.

See within a manger laid
Jesus, Lord of heaven and earth.

Gloria in excelsis Deo!
Gloria in excelsis Deo!

Angels we have heard on high
Sweetly singing o'er the plains.

We sing Gloria.

O COME, ALL YE FAITHFUL

BIBLE POINT:

God's plan is something to celebrate.

KEY SCRIPTURES: The Shepherds Tell About Jesus' Birth (Luke 2:14-20; John 1:12, 14)

FOR LEADERS

An invitation just arrived in the mail. Your niece is graduating, or your college roommate is getting married. Perhaps your child's friend is having a birthday party, or it's your grandparents' 60th anniversary. Regardless of the event, there's reason for celebration and *you're* invited!

Kids like to party with the best of them! A party invitation brings excitement and anticipation—someone wants *them* to join the fun. Perhaps the shepherds shared that joy when they RSVP'd "yes" to an invitation to go see the Savior. It was an interesting guest list—shepherds fresh from the field, a young mom, a carpenter, and travelers' animals. But Jesus was there, so let the party begin! **God's plan is something to celebrate**. Use this lesson to invite kids to receive and respond to the best invitation ever—to be friends with Jesus!

We're invited to friendship with Jesus throughout the New Testament of the Bible. As you prepare for this lesson, read these passages so their welcoming words are fresh in your mind and heart: Matthew 11:28; Ephesians 2:18; 1 Corinthians 1:9. Pray for Jesus to provide opportunities to share his invitation with your kids.

OVERVIEW

EXPERIENCES		ACTIVITIES	SUPPLIES
Get Started	15 minutes	Share about fun parties and play a party game.	• Christmas candy or trinkets (1 per child) • box • 2 designs of wrapping paper • music player • Christmas music
Bible Discovery	10 minutes	**You're Invited!**—Make an invitation to celebrate Jesus.	• Bibles • "You're Invited!" handout copied on multicolored card stock (1 for every 2 kids) • markers and crayons
	10-15 minutes	**Party Planning**—Plan a party, and see how Jesus is everything we need.	• Bibles • catalogs, grocery ads, department store ads • whiteboard or poster board • marker • scissors • tape
	10-15 minutes	**After Party**—See what people did after Jesus' party was over.	• Bibles
Music Video	3 minutes	Sing "O Come, All Ye Faithful."	• "O Come, All Ye Faithful" music video
Carol Story: "O Come, All Ye Faithful"	10 minutes	Practice copying music like John Francis Wade.	• paper (1 piece per child) • pencils (1 per child)
Life Application and Prayer	10-15 minutes	Design an invitation to help tell someone about Jesus' birth.	• invitations from "You're Invited!" activity • markers, crayons • ribbon • washi tape

⇨ GET STARTED

Welcome kids with music! Play and sing along with the "Angels We Have Heard on High" and "O Come, All Ye Faithful" music videos as kids gather.

Get kids talking with this icebreaker question.

Ask: **What's the best party you ever went to? What made it so special?** Share an example from your own life to begin the conversation. Then let kids share with their friends until you're ready to begin the lesson.

Say: **Parties and celebrations are so fun! But you typically don't just show up uninvited. The host sends invitations that ask you to come. The message says, "Please come. There's a spot for you!"**

For the very first Christmas party, the angels invited the shepherds to come see and celebrate Jesus' birth. While we might not get a heavenly invitation from angels, we're invited to celebrate Jesus, too. Through Jesus, God says, "Please come close to me. There's a spot in my family for you!" Wow! <u>God's plan is something to celebrate</u>.

One of the best things about parties is that you get to play games. Let's start our time together with a party game.

To prepare for this game, place individually wrapped Christmas candy or trinkets in a box. This is a great way to distribute Christmas gifts to your kids! When everything is in the box, wrap it multiple times with alternating wrapping-paper designs. Add at least five layers. The more layers you wrap, the longer the game will last.

Have kids form a circle. Show them the wrapped Christmas present, and tell them there's something inside for everyone. Play Christmas music as kids pass the present around the circle. At random intervals, turn off the music. When the music stops, whoever's holding the present will unwrap just one layer of wrapping paper. Play music again, and have kids resume passing the present. Continue until the gift is completely unwrapped. Encourage the child who opens the box to share the treats with all the kids.

This is a great time to play the Christmas songs from previous lessons!

Say: **Just like our gift had something for all of us, friendship with Jesus is for everyone. When we say yes to Jesus' friendship invitation, we become children of**

God! John 1:12 says it like this: "But to all who believed him and accepted him, he gave the right to become children of God."

Let's explore what happened after the angels invited shepherds to go meet Jesus. As we read, we'll make invitations for celebrating Jesus' birth.

🔭 BIBLE DISCOVERY

YOU'RE INVITED!

Copy the "You're Invited!" handout onto brightly colored card stock. Cut the handout in half, and give each child a blank invitation.

Say: **The last several verses of the Christmas story give us all the information we need to fill out this invitation. We'll discover the details and then decorate the invitations to give to someone at the end of our time together.**

Have a volunteer read Luke 2:15.

The shepherds decided to go to Bethlehem and find the celebration. Encourage kids to write "Bethlehem" on the line beside "Where" on their invitations. Be ready to help younger kids with spelling. **When you respond to an invitation, you say whether you're coming or not. The shepherds said "yes." They wanted to see this baby who made the armies of heaven celebrate. Jesus was the reason for the party. In Luke 2:11, the angel of the Lord told them that the Messiah had been born. The *Messiah* is someone who saves or rescues.**

Ask: **Why do you think the shepherds were so excited to see Jesus?**

We aren't sure what the shepherds knew about the promised Messiah or what they expected him to do, but we do know they were eager to see him. They must have expected something amazing!

Ask: **If you were inviting someone to meet Jesus, what would you say?** Share your own ideas to begin. After kids share, have them write a response on the line beside "Celebrating What" on their invitations. Encourage them to use their own words, and be ready to help kids with spelling. Ideas include:

- Come meet Jesus!
- Come see the baby.
- Come see how much God loves you!
- Come meet your best friend!

We've written where the shepherds were going and what they were celebrating. You can set your invitations to the side for now. We'll come back to them later. Let's keep reading to find out what the party was like.

PARTY PLANNING

Ask: **What do you usually find at a party or celebration?** Invite kids' ideas. Then divide kids into four groups or party-planning committees.

Say: **Let's pretend that we are planning a party to celebrate Jesus' birth. Each group is a party-planning committee in charge of something different.**

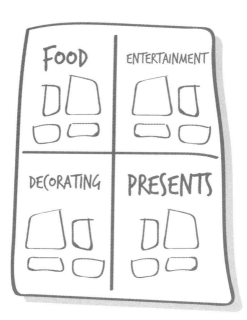

Designate a Food Team, Entertainment Team, Decorating Team, and Presents Team. Provide party supply catalogs, grocery store ads, and department store ads to each group. Each group will plan its part of the celebration, choosing and cutting out at least four pictures or drawings to show the ideas.

While groups work, divide a whiteboard or large piece of poster board into four sections, and label each section with one of the committee names.

After about five minutes, groups will present their ideas and tape the pictures to their sections of the board. After all groups have shared, review the party plans with the whole group. There may be some unexpected ideas!

Have a volunteer read Luke 2:16.

The shepherds found Mary, Joseph, and Jesus in a stable. The Bible doesn't mention any food, decorations, games, or presents—until the wise men arrived a little later.

A simple barn with a family staying in it may not seem like much of a party, but Jesus was everything they needed and more! Let's see how he helps each party-planning section.

Point to the Food section, and write "Jesus" over the top of the pictures.

Friendship with Jesus satisfies us. When we feel like something is missing in our lives, Jesus is with us and fills us with his love.

Ask: **Tell about a time Jesus gave you what you needed.** Share an example from your own life to begin. Perhaps you needed a friend to talk to, so you wrote down a prayer to Jesus and felt better, or maybe Jesus used a hug from someone to show you his love.

Point to the Decorating section, and write "Jesus" over the top of the pictures.

When we're friends with Jesus, we see beautiful things around us differently. We notice things in nature like flowers, clouds in the sky, or big trees, and we know that all those beautiful things come from him.

Ask: **Tell about something beautiful you've seen.** Share an example from your own life to begin. Perhaps it was a rainbow, a sunset, or a flower.

Point to the Entertainment section, and write "Jesus" over the top of the pictures.

Being Jesus' friend is fun! It may sound strange because we can't actually see Jesus. We can't ask him to be on our team or laugh at his jokes. But the joy we feel during happy times comes from him. Without Jesus, we'd be sad and stuck in our selfishness and sin. But since he rescued us from sin, we can have joy!

Ask: **What brings you joy?** Have kids think of something that makes them happy and then all shout it out on the count of three. Repeat several times, encouraging kids to shout joyfully and with enthusiasm.

Point to the Presents section, and write "Jesus" over the top of the pictures.

Friendship with Jesus is a gift from God. Because of God's great love, we can live as Jesus' friends forever. It's not a present that we open once, enjoy, and then never use again. When we're friends with Jesus, there's always more to discover about him. He grows up with us and never leaves us. Now *that's* something to celebrate! Let's see how the people at Jesus' first party celebrated after they met him.

AFTER PARTY

Read Luke 2:17-19.

Say: **The shepherds loved Jesus' Christmas party so much that they wanted other people to know about it. When people heard, they were astonished. That means they were amazed. They were flabbergasted by the shepherds' message.**

Ask: **Why do you think people were so surprised? Tell about a time you were shocked and amazed.** Share a story from your own life to begin.

We don't know what people did after they heard about Jesus. Did they really believe the shepherds? Did they go to see him, too? Or did they snap out of it and go on with life as usual? We don't know. But we do know how Mary responded. Verse 19 says she "kept all these things in her heart and thought about them often."

Encourage kids to think about something they treasure. Perhaps it's a gift they just received, a stuffed animal, or something they collect.

Ask: **Turn to a partner and tell about something you treasure. Where do you keep that cherished possession?** Share an example to start.

When we treasure something, we love it and keep it in a safe place. For Mary, she treasured Jesus and his birth celebration, and she kept that treasure in her heart. I imagine Mary thought back on that day with a lot of joy and love. Let's read about what the shepherds did after they met Jesus.

Read Luke 2:20.

Every party ends sometime. The shepherds went back to their flocks—after all, they couldn't just leave the sheep alone on the hillside! But they didn't stop celebrating Jesus and praising God. The plan that the angel had told them about was true. God's plan is something to celebrate!

God still invites us to meet Jesus today. We might not travel to Bethlehem, but we can come to church and meet him through friends and leaders. We meet him when we read about him in the Bible. We hear about how friendship with Jesus helps people during difficult times, and we can talk to Jesus about things we go through in life. God invites us—"come faithful friends!" Come spend time with Jesus! Let's sing a song that reminds us that God's plan is something to celebrate!

♪♪♪ MUSIC VIDEO

Play the "O Come, All Ye Faithful" music video, and encourage kids to sing along and do the motions. They'll really have a blast if you lead the way!

📖 CAROL STORY: "O COME, ALL YE FAITHFUL"

Say: **Imagine when there were no copy machines or computers. When someone wrote a story or poem, you couldn't just make copies to share with others. You couldn't just share something on Instagram or Facebook. There were no copy machines, but there *were* human copyists. John Francis Wade was one of them. He was born in England and then moved to a town in France. John Francis' job was to copy and sell music. He copied a lot of music for churches. He must have had very good handwriting because we can still read his first copies of "O Come, All Ye Faithful" from almost 300 years ago! Some people think John Francis was a musician who wrote his own songs, too. The song "O Come, All Ye Faithful" made him famous.**

Invite kids to practice being a copyist. Give them each a piece of paper, and have them write the first line of "O Come, All Ye Faithful" two times. Have kids try their best to make the copies look exactly the same (without tracing). Encourage them to sign their name at the bottom of each copy.

We know that John Francis copied the earliest versions of "O Come, All Ye Faithful" because he signed his name at the bottom. Through the years, other people added different words and melodies. Eventually, the version we sing now was included in church hymnals that were copied, not by hand but at a printing press. Like the shepherds, John Francis' Christmas song spread the good news of Jesus' birth!

Whether he wrote the whole song, parts of it, or just copied down a song other people already knew, John Francis' song "O Come, All Ye Faithful" helps people celebrate Jesus' birth by telling the story and inviting people to meet Jesus!

One line from the song comes from another verse in John.

Read John 1:14.

"The Word" is another name for Jesus. He loves us, and he is faithful. When people are faithful, that means they're committed and they don't quit. Jesus will always be our friend. We can be his faithful friends, too, and celebrate his birth.

LIFE APPLICATION AND PRAYER

Say: **God invites us to meet and become friends with Jesus. At Christmas, we celebrate that Jesus came to be our Rescuer and save us from sin. Even though almost everyone celebrates or knows about *Christmas*, not everyone celebrates and knows *Jesus*. Like the angels invited the shepherds to celebrate Jesus, we can invite others to meet him, too. We share Jesus with our words, like John Francis Wade, and with our lives. Jesus' friends show other people what his love and friendship look like. People can meet him through us!**

Pray and thank Jesus for inviting us to be his friends. Ask for his help as we share his friendship with others.

Invite kids to add finishing touches to their invitations. They can add additional details and decorate the invitations with ribbon, washi tape, markers, or crayons. Encourage kids to use the invitations to share the Christmas story with friends or family members.

If time remains, keep singing! We recommend "Joy to the World!" or "Silent Night."

TAKE IT HOME

Distribute the take-home page for this lesson to each child, or email the page to families.

YOU'RE INVITED!

GLORY TO GOD!

Please help us celebrate.

Where: _____

Celebrating What: _____

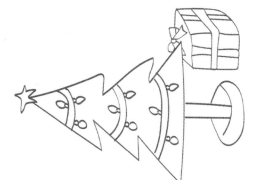

"LET'S GO TO BETHLEHEM! LET'S SEE THIS THING THAT HAS HAPPENED, WHICH THE LORD HAS TOLD US ABOUT" (Luke 2:15).

YOU'RE INVITED!

GLORY TO GOD!

Please help us celebrate.

Where: _____

Celebrating What: _____

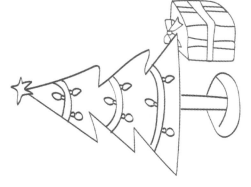

"LET'S GO TO BETHLEHEM! LET'S SEE THIS THING THAT HAS HAPPENED, WHICH THE LORD HAS TOLD US ABOUT" (Luke 2:15).

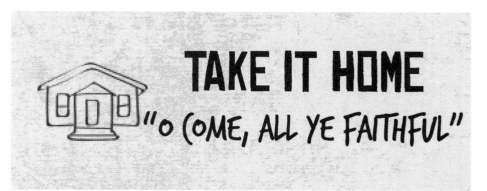

DISCOVER

God's plan is something to celebrate.

READ

Luke 2:15-20

Parties and celebrations are so fun, but you typically don't just show up uninvited. The hosts send invitations that ask you to come. Their message says, "Please come. There's a spot for you!"

For the very first Christmas party, the angels invited the shepherds to come see and celebrate Jesus' birth. While we might not get a heavenly invitation from angels, we're invited to celebrate Jesus, too. Through Jesus, God says, "Please come close to me. There's a spot in my family for you!" Wow! God's plan is something to celebrate.

SHARE

Throw an impromptu party with your family. Make decorations, prepare snacks, and choose games. While you're together, think back on the Christmas season and talk about this:

What's your favorite thing we did to celebrate Christmas this year?

What do you think was Jesus' favorite thing we did to celebrate his birthday?

PRAY

When everyone has shared, pray and thank Jesus for being with your family as you celebrate his birthday.

LISTEN

Count the number of times you randomly hear "O Come, All Ye Faithful" this week. It may be on your car radio or music you hear in stores or on TV. You can keep track on a phone or notebook. Which Christmas song have you heard the most?

SONGS OF THE CHRISTMAS STORY

SONG LYRICS
"O COME, ALL YE FAITHFUL"

O come, all ye faithful,
Joyful, and triumphant.
O come ye, O come ye to Bethlehem.
Come and behold him,
Born the King of angels.

O come, let us adore him.
O come, let us adore him.
O come, let us adore him,
Christ the Lord.

Yea, Lord, we greet thee,
Born this happy morning.
Jesus, to thee be all glory given;
Word of the Father, now in flesh appearing.

O come, let us adore him.
O come, let us adore him.
O come, let us adore him,
Christ the Lord.

O come, all ye faithful,
Joyful, and triumphant.

O come, let us adore him.
O come, let us adore him.
O come, let us adore him,
Christ the Lord.

O come, let us adore.

"O Come, All Ye Faithful" by John F. Wade.

Group
Real. Bold. Love.

WANT MORE QUICK CHILDREN'S MINISTRY LESSONS?

KIDMIN QUICK PICKS are the perfect solution!

These easy-to-use, downloadable lessons are packed with interactive learning experiences, fun activities, media, and thought-provoking discussion questions that'll deepen kids' faith.

EACH VERSATILE 4-WEEK LESSON PACK INCLUDES...

4 complete, Bible-based lessons

4 Parent Pages to give parents a starting point to talk with their kids about what they learned or discovered

Teaching Video to illustrate lesson points and let kids explore faith points more deeply

Countdown Video for the start of each lesson time

Graphics Pack with lesson helps, plus publicity tools and media templates so you can spread the word about your series

- Promotional Poster (11x17)
- Editable Bulletin Insert
- 2 Slides (for lessons notes, points, or promotions)
- Email Header
- Facebook | Instagram | Twitter Images

TO SEE THE ENTIRE SERIES, VISIT GROUP.COM/QUICKPICKS